# The **Food Poisoning** Update

Alvin and Virginia Silverstein and Laura Silverstein Nunn

## Titles in the DISEASE UPDATE series:

The AIDS Update
ISBN-13: 978-0-7660-2746-6
ISBN-10:   0-7660-2746-5

The Asthma Update
ISBN-13: 978-0-7660-2482-3
ISBN-10:   0-7660-2482-2

The Breast Cancer Update
ISBN-13: 978-0-7660-2747-3
ISBN-10:   0-7660-2747-3

The Diabetes Update
ISBN-13: 978-0-7660-2483-0
ISBN-10:   0-7660-2483-0

The Flu and Pneumonia Update
ISBN-13: 978-0-7660-2480-9
ISBN-10:   0-7660-2480-6

The Food Poisoning Update
ISBN-13: 978-0-7660-2748-0
ISBN-10:   0-7660-2748-1

The Sickle Cell Anemia Update
ISBN-13: 978-0-7660-2479-3
ISBN-10:   0-7660-2479-2

The STDs Update
ISBN-13: 978-0-7660-2484-7
ISBN-10:   0-7660-2484-9

The Tuberculosis Update
ISBN-13: 978-0-7660-2481-6
ISBN-10:   0-7660-2481-4

DISEASE
UPDATE

# The **Food Poisoning** Update

Alvin and Virginia Silverstein and Laura Silverstein Nunn

**Enslow Publishers, Inc.**
40 Industrial Road
Box 398
Berkeley Heights, NJ 07922
USA
            http://www.enslow.com

**Acknowledgments**

The authors thank Dr. Lynne A. McLandsborough, Associate Professor of Food Microbiology at University of Massachusetts Amherst, and Dr. Stanley E. Katz, Professor of Microbiology at Rutgers University, NJ, for their careful reading of the manuscript and their many helpful comments and suggestions.

**Library of Congress Cataloging-in-Publication Data**

Silverstein, Alvin.

    The food poisoning update / Alvin and Virginia Silverstein and Laura Silverstein Nunn.

       p. cm.— (Disease update)

    Includes bibliographical references and index.

    ISBN-13: 978-0-7660-2748-0

    ISBN-10: 0-7660-2748-1

       1. Food poisoning—Juvenile literature. I. Silverstein, Virginia B. II. Nunn, Laura Silverstein. III. Title.

    RC143.S55 2007

    615.9'54—dc22

                          2006032822

Printed in the United States of America

10 9 8 7 6 5 4 3 2 1

**To Our Readers:** We have done our best to make sure all Internet Addresses in this book were active and appropriate when we went to press. However, the author and the publisher have no control over and assume no liability for the material available on those Internet sites or on other Web sites they may link to. Any comments or suggestions can be sent by e-mail to comments@enslow.com or to the address on the back cover.

**Photo Credits:** Aaron Haupt/Photo Researchers, Inc., p. 78; AJPhoto/Photo Researchers, Inc., p. 91; Associated Press, pp. 33, 50, 56, 65; © Bettman/CORBIS, p. 16; Courtesy of Dr. Carl Winter, p.100; CNRI/Photo Researchers, Inc., p. 37 (shigella); © Corel Corporation, p. 55; Pr. Courtieu/Photo Researchers, Inc., p. 37 (listeria); David Young-Wolff/Photo Edit, pp. 46, 79; Explorer/PhotoResearchers, Inc., p. 25 (Pasteur), 108; Eye of Science/Photo Researchers, Inc., pp. 5, 13, 37 (e. coli), 109; Giraudon/Art Resource, NY, p. 20; The Granger Collection, New York, p. 27 (artwork); Ingram Publishing, p. 85; © Jupiterimages Corporation, pp. 3, 35, 42, 62, 69, 72; Library of Congress, Prints & Photographs Division, FSA-OWI Collection, reproduction number LC-USE6-D-003449 DLC, p. 21; NASA, p. 97; © 2006 Los Angeles Times, reprinted with permission, p. 31; Mary Kate Denny/Photo Edit, p. 93; Michael Newman/Photo Edit, p. 77; M.I. Walker/Photo Researchers, Inc., p. 37 (clostridium botulinum); National Agricultural Library, p. 25 (poster); National Cancer Institute, p. 40; The New York American, 1909, p. 19; New York City Municipal Archives, p. 18; Partnership for Food Safety Education, p. 95; Pascal Goetgheluck/Photo Researchers, Inc., p. 67; Shutterstock, pp. 8, 53, 89, 94; USDA, pp. 37 (campylobacter), 76, 87; USDA/Science Source, p. 37 (salmonella); Wellcome Library, London, p. 27 (poster).

**Cover Photos (clockwise from top left):** USDA/Science Source; Shutterstock; Eye of Science/Photo Researchers, Inc.; © Jupiterimages Corporation.

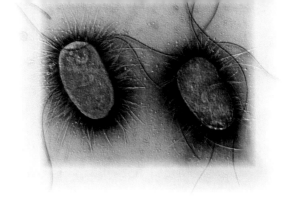

# Contents

# Food Poisoning

### What is it?
An illness caused by consuming food or drink that has been contaminated with disease-causing germs (bacteria or viruses), parasites, toxins, or chemicals.

### Who gets it?
Anyone can get it, both males and females, and any ethnic group. An estimated 76 million Americans get food poisoning every year. Young children, the elderly, and people with weakened immune systems are the most vulnerable to the illness.

### What are the symptoms?
Food poisoning can have many different causes, so the symptoms can vary greatly. Common symptoms include nausea, abdominal pain, vomiting, diarrhea, fever, headache, or tiredness.

### How is it treated?
In most cases, the treatment is bed rest and replacing lost fluids. More serious cases may need medical attention.

### How can it be prevented?
Wash hands and food surfaces with soap and water before and after handling fresh meat, poultry, or fish, and after using the bathroom. Meat, poultry, fish, and eggs should be cooked thoroughly. Keep hot foods hot and cold foods cold.

A catered lunch was the beginning of a food poisoning outbreak at a Teacher Appreciation event.

# 1

# Was It Something You Ate?

I N MAY 2006, TEACHERS from New Jersey's Readington Township middle school were looking forward to their annual luncheon during Teacher Appreciation Week. A local restaurant was catering the event, supplying chicken, eggplant parmigiana, penne pasta, and a green salad with dressing. Parents volunteered to bring desserts. Everything went as planned, and the teachers enjoyed the food. Two days later, however, about thirty-five of the fifty teachers who attended the luncheon called in sick. They all seemed to have the same symptoms: vomiting, nausea, diarrhea, and stomach pains. School officials soon realized that this was more than an odd coincidence. They suspected food poisoning and notified the county health department.

When health officials came on the scene, they investigated a number of possible causes. They ruled out the district's cafeteria and wells because none of the students had gotten sick. They interviewed more than one hundred staff members and gave them detailed questionnaires to fill out. They also collected samples of some food left over from the teachers' luncheon, as well as stool (feces) samples from some of those who got sick.

Nothing showed up in the samples of leftover food, which could be tested only for bacteria. The test results from the stool samples, however, showed that the food poisoning was caused by a very contagious type of norovirus. Just a tiny amount of this virus can spread easily from person to person, especially in the crowded conditions of a faculty luncheon. But how did it get there? Health officials visited the restaurant that catered the luncheon. It was an unannounced inspection to see if the workers used the basic food safety practices. Everything turned out to be normal. The restaurant also did not have any reports of sick customers or employees. The health officials crossed the restaurant off the list of possible causes of the outbreak.

Analyzing the questionnaires that staff members had filled out revealed the connecting link: All the people who got sick ate the green salad. John Beckley, director of the county health department believed that the virus might not have been in the food itself. He said it could have been on a utensil used to serve the salad. If someone who had the virus handled a spoon, everybody who picked up the spoon would pick up the virus.[1] He also said that people can carry the virus without having any symptoms, so they can easily spread it to others without even knowing. Health officials told everyone involved in the luncheon that the best way to stop the virus from spreading was to wash their hands regularly and to disinfect surfaces in their homes.

Many food poisoning mysteries never get solved. In this case, however, they were lucky because the principal notified the health department immediately. The health department staff worked overtime to collect samples and interview the sick teachers while the outbreak was actually going on. If there had been a delay, the virus might not have shown up in their stool samples, and people might not have remembered exactly what they ate.[2]

Everybody gets stomachaches at one time or another. Sometimes they are caused by eating too much. Some people get them when they eat a food that "doesn't agree with them." But when two or more people are having stomach problems after eating the same food, it could be a sign of food poisoning. Food poisoning is an illness that happens when people consume food or drink that has been contaminated with harmful chemicals or disease-causing creatures, such as bacteria, viruses, or parasites. Some bacteria send out toxins (poisons) that can make food go bad. Others produce toxins while they are multiplying in a person's body. Some foods, such as certain kinds of

> Food poisoning is an illness that happens when people consume food or drink that has been contaminated with harmful chemicals or disease-causing creatures, such as bacteria, viruses, or parasites.

mushrooms and fish, naturally contain poisonous chemicals that can make people sick.

Medical experts often use the term *foodborne illness* for cases of food poisoning, especially those caused by bacteria and other microorganisms. Although the food supply in the United States is one of the safest in the world, food poisoning is fairly common. According to the Centers for Disease Control and

## Blame It on Germs

Most cases of food poisoning are caused by bacteria or viruses. These germs are microorganisms—tiny creatures that cannot be seen without a microscope. Viruses are even smaller than bacteria. They can live only in people and other

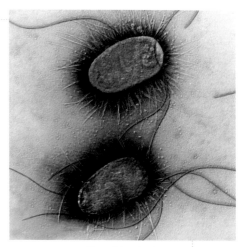

*E. coli* bacteria

living things. Diseases such as colds, flu, and chickenpox are caused by viruses. Bacteria are everywhere—on human skin, inside the body, in the air, in food and water, and on everything we touch. Most of them do not cause any harm. In fact, some are even helpful. Bacteria in our intestines, for example, help to digest our food and make vitamins for us. Sometimes, though, even normally harmless microorganisms can make us sick. Under the right conditions—warmth, moisture, and plenty of food—germs can multiply to harmful levels.

Prevention (CDC), every year an estimated 76 million Americans get sick from something they ate. Nearly 325,000 of them need to be hospitalized, and more than 5,000 die from eating contaminated food.[3]

Most cases of food poisoning are mild and will go away after a couple of days. For this reason, many people do not seek medical help. Sometimes, however, the illness can last for days, even weeks. When symptoms become more serious, a trip to the hospital is necessary. In some very rare cases, food poisoning may lead to death.

There is no way to guarantee that the food we eat is completely safe. However, by following a number of food safety guidelines, we can greatly reduce the chances of getting food poisoning.

# 2

# Food Poisoning in History

I N THE LATE 1800s, Mary Mallon came to America from Ireland to work as a cook for wealthy families. In the summer of 1906, she was hired to work for New York banker Charles Henry Warren and his family in a summer vacation home they rented in Oyster Bay, Long Island.

On August 27, one of the Warren daughters came down with typhoid fever. (Typhoid is an illness caused by a salmonella bacterium that is spread through food or water. The bacterium attacks a person's intestines and may cause a high fever, headache, diarrhea, and extreme tiredness.) Within a short time, six out of eleven people in the household had come down with typhoid fever.

That winter, George Soper, a sanitary engineer who had experience with typhoid outbreaks, tested the water sources. He did not find any disease-causing organisms. He then focused on the cook, Mary Mallon, as a possible source of contamination. By that time, Mallon was no longer working for the Warrens; she had left them about three weeks after the outbreak. Soper discovered that among the seven families for whom Mallon had worked between 1900 and 1907,

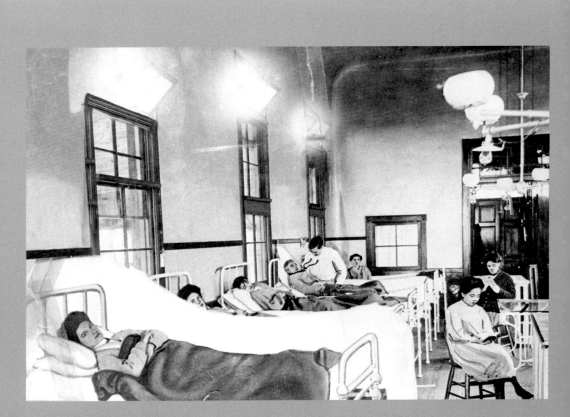

Mary Mallon (front left) was known as Typhoid Mary. She was hospitalized to prevent her from spreading typhoid while working as a cook in New York.

twenty-two people had become ill with typhoid fever. Soper was convinced he was on the right track. The next thing he needed to do was to get samples of Mallon's blood and stool (feces) to prove that she had spread the disease.

With the help of police, Mallon was taken to the Willard Parker Hospital in New York, where samples of her blood and stool were collected. Tests of the samples showed typhoid bacteria in her stool. It was clear that Mallon was a carrier—she had spread the typhoid bacterium to other people even though she did not have any symptoms. Not everyone with typhoid becomes very ill. It is possible that Mallon might have had a mild case of typhoid and thought she had a touch of the flu. After she recovered, some typhoid bacteria remained in her body and continued to come out in her stool. She most likely spread the disease when she cooked for people with unwashed hands after going to the bathroom. Unfortunately, no one at the time explained all the facts to Mary Mallon, and she continued to feel that she was being falsely accused.

Mallon was kept under house arrest in an isolated cottage for the next three years without having had a trial. By this time, people were calling her Typhoid

Mary Mallon was quarantined in this isolated cottage on an island in New York's East River from 1907 to 1910, and again from 1915 until she died.

Mary. In 1910, a new health commissioner decided to give Mallon her freedom as long as she agreed not to work as a cook again. Mallon agreed and was released.

In January 1915, there was a typhoid outbreak in Manhattan. Twenty-five people got sick, and two of them died. Evidence pointed to a cook named Mrs. Brown—who turned out to be Mary Mallon, using a fake name. Mallon never believed that she was spreading the disease. She was sent back into isolation, where she stayed for the next twenty-three years. All in

This 1909 illustration shows Typhoid Mary spreading typhoid, and her stay in the hospital.

all, Typhoid Mary was linked to about fifty cases of typhoid fever; three of the patients died.[1]

### Food Safety Through the Ages

Food safety has been a major concern for humans throughout history—since long before Mary Mallon's time. In ancient times, people often got sick from eating spoiled food. Early on, they learned that animals killed for food had to be eaten right away before the meat

Wedding banquet scene from the late middle ages.

## Food Tasters

During the Middle Ages (about A.D. 500 to 1500), poisons hidden in food were commonly used as a weapon. To prevent assassination attempts on an important person, such as an emperor or monarch, it was common for Royal Courts to use "food tasters"—people who ate a sample of the food first to make sure it was not poisoned. If the food taster survived, then the food was safe to eat. However, this test was not very useful for slow-acting poisons, which take a long time to do their damage.

went "bad." Soon people figured out how to use nature's tools to preserve food so that they could eat it at a later time. For example, in cold climates, meat was packed in ice to keep it frozen. In warm climates, foods were dried in the sun. During the Middle Ages, the Romans built "still houses" (much like greenhouses) in which they could dry fruits, vegetables, and herbs in areas where the sun was not strong enough for drying.

In the 1600s, wealthy Americans and food sellers such as butchers had icehouses built to store their ice and to keep their food frozen. In the early 1800s, the icebox was invented, and people could then store food *inside* their home. However, people with iceboxes had to receive regular deliveries of ice to keep their icebox cold. In the late 1800s, the first mechanical refrigerator was invented. It had its own built-in cooling system, which

Refrigerators became common in the 1930s. This refrigerator is from 1942. Keeping food cold is an important way to limit the growth of disease-causing bacteria.

eliminated the need for ice deliveries. By the early 1930s, refrigerators had become common in American homes.

An important breakthrough in food preservation took place in the 1790s. Nicolas Appert, a French confectioner, discovered that food heated and sealed in airtight glass bottles could be stored safely for days, months, or even years. Around 1806, Appert tested his

Canning has proved to be a successful method of protecting and preserving food.

discovery on Napoléon Bonaparte's French army. It was not uncommon for men in the military to get sick, and even die, from spoiled food. Appert was able to supply them with a wide variety of foods, including meat, vegetables, fruit, and milk. The test was a success—no one got sick.

In 1810, Englishman Peter Durand made an important change in Appert's methods: He developed a process that sealed food into unbreakable metal containers—cans. The first commercial canning factory was set up in England in 1813. The cans were lighter than glass bottles, easier to seal, and less likely to get damaged during storage and transportation.

Canning has proved to be a successful method of protecting and preserving food. If the food is not heated high enough or long enough during the canning process, however, canning does not protect against one important form of food poisoning: botulism.

## The Mystery of Sausage Poisoning

Botulism is the deadliest form of food poisoning in history. The first reported outbreak was in 1793, in Wildbad, Germany. It affected thirteen people, killing six of them, after they ate contaminated blood sausage. Sausage was made by filling a pig's intestines with meat and blood and boiling it in water. After that, it was stored at room temperature. As more and more people fell ill, a local doctor, Justinius Kerner, decided to do his own research into this "sausage poisoning," as he called it. In 1829, he published a report describing 230 cases, in which most of the patients had eaten sausage. Kerner wrote about the sausage poison, which had devastating effects on the nervous system. Patients had blurred vision and dry mouth; it was hard for them to swallow and to speak clearly. They suffered from muscle weakness, which developed into paralysis. In severe cases, the poison paralyzed the respiratory muscles, making it hard to breathe and ultimately leading to death.

Sausage poisoning was named botulism, from *botulus,* which is Latin for "sausage." Although Kerner made a detailed study of the disease, he was not able to determine exactly what caused it. At that time, people did not realize that invisible "germs" could cause diseases.

## Bacteria and Disease

It was not until the mid-1800s that a link was made between bacteria and disease. In 1857, French chemist Louis Pasteur showed that milk turned sour because microorganisms were growing in it. Starting in the early 1860s, Pasteur conducted experiments in which he used heat to kill the harmful microorganisms in beer and wine. He found that the wine-spoiling creatures could be destroyed by heating the wine to 135°F (57°F). Harmful microorganisms in milk were destroyed when the milk was heated to 161°F (72°C). This process, now called pasteurization, was named after Louis Pasteur. By 1917, most major American cities had laws that required milk to be pasteurized.

In 1878, Louis Pasteur published a paper detailing his "germ theory" of disease. He proposed that many diseases are caused by tiny microorganisms, like those that grow in milk and wine. Pasteur's discoveries made a huge impact on the medical community. However, he was not able to identify the germs that caused the various diseases, as he had hoped to do. German physician Robert Koch, on the other hand, developed methods for

The process of pasteurization was named after Louis Pasteur, the French chemist and biologist. Pasteurization kills the harmful bacteria in milk and juice.

In 1878, Louis Pasteur proposed that many diseases are caused by tiny microorganisms.

growing bacteria in a laboratory. He used staining techniques that allowed him to identify germs. He also laid out specific procedures that had to be followed in order to prove that certain bacteria caused certain diseases. In 1876, Koch identified the first bacterium to be linked to a particular disease—anthrax. Anthrax is a disease that usually affects animals, but it can be transmitted to humans. In 1882, he discovered the bacterium that causes tuberculosis. Then in 1883, while he was in Egypt investigating a cholera outbreak, he discovered the bacterium that causes the foodborne illness cholera.

The linking of germs with diseases also made it possible to determine the cause of botulism. In 1895, a group of musicians played at a funeral in Belgium. Within a day or two, twenty-three of the thirty-four musicians became seriously ill. They had double vision, difficulty swallowing, and muscle paralysis. Three of them died. A Belgian doctor, Emile van Ermengem, investigated the outbreak and learned that the musicians had eaten a meal of pickled and smoked ham after the funeral. Van Ermengem fed some of the ham to

## Bad Water on Broad Street

When a cholera outbreak hit London in 1854, health officials blamed it on "bad air." It was a common belief that this disease affected only poor people and was brought on by unclean conditions in overpopulated areas. Throughout history,  cholera had been a devastating disease, causing severe diarrhea, dehydration (serious water loss), fever, and often death.

John Snow, a physician, started his own investigation into the cholera outbreak. After mapping out each cholera case, Snow noticed that most of the cases—with about 500 deaths in just ten days—occurred in one neighborhood.[2] These people had one main thing in common: They all got their water from the Broad Street pump. It seemed obvious to Snow that the water from the Broad Street pump was somehow infecting people with cholera.

Snow convinced local officials to remove the handle from the Broad Street pump. This forced the residents to get their water from another pump. The number of cholera cases dropped

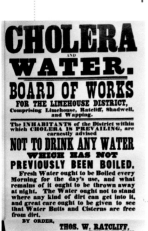

immediately. Snow later uncovered the source of the problem. Apparently, the water company that supplied the Broad Street pump got their supply from the Thames River, which had been heavily polluted with raw sewage.

John Snow did not show that germs caused cholera, but he did show how quickly disease can spread through a population.

laboratory animals, and they came down with the same symptoms as the musicians. Then he isolated bacteria from samples of the ham and from the victims. Van Ermengem continued to study these bacteria, which are now known as *Clostridium botulinum.* He found that these microorganisms grow and multiply only under oxygen-free conditions, such as in a sausage (covered by an airtight casing) or in canned foods. As they grow, the bacteria produce a powerful toxin (poison), which remains in the food. Van Ermengem advised that food be cooked properly, and any food that looks or smells bad should be thrown out. This is still good advice today.

# 3

# What Is Food Poisoning?

NINE-YEAR-OLD BRIANNE KINER was excited to hear that her dad was picking up some burgers for dinner at a Jack in the Box® restaurant near her Seattle home. She loved cheeseburgers, so she didn't mind that this was the second time in one week she was dining on cheeseburgers from one of her favorite fast-food restaurants. Within a couple of days, Brianne and her sister, Karin, started to develop flulike symptoms and diarrhea. Karin started to feel better, but Brianne's illness got worse. She had painful abdominal cramps, and her diarrhea became bloody. Brianne's parents took her to the hospital.

Health officials discovered that Brianne's sickness was caused by undercooked burgers from Jack in the

Box. As it turned out, the burgers contained a dangerous type of bacteria called *Escherichia coli* O157:H7, or *E. coli* O157:H7 for short. *E. coli* can be found in the intestines of warm-blooded animals. Most strains of *E. coli* are not harmful, but this particular one—*E. coli* O157:H7—produces a powerful toxin that can cause serious damage to the intestine, kidneys, and other important organs. That is what had happened to Brianne.

Brianne spent more than six months in the hospital, part of the time in a coma. Her mother was told many times that her daughter was going to die. But Brianne did wake up from her coma after nearly six weeks and continued to get stronger. However, the *E. coli* bacteria had already caused a great deal of trouble for the girl. During her hospital stay, she had three strokes and more than 10,000 seizures. Her large intestine was so damaged that doctors had to remove much of it. Her pancreas was also damaged, making it difficult for her body to use sugar properly, so she had to take medicine for diabetes. Doctors say that Brianne will also need a kidney transplant in the future.

Brianne Kiner was one of more than seven hundred people across four states affected by the *E. coli*-tainted

Suzanne Kiner (left) and her daughter Brianne Kiner, now 23. Brianne continues to battle health problems related to an *E. coli* poisoning after eating contaminated hamburgers.

Jack in the Box burgers in 1993. Before this outbreak, few people knew much about *E. coli*. That changed when news about the Jack in the Box *E. coli* poisoning made it to newspapers and TV all over the country.

Even as a young adult, Brianne still has health problems stemming from the *E. coli* infection. But she is a strong person with a positive attitude. Despite what she has been through, she still loves to eat hamburgers, but now she's a little more cautious. "I just make sure the burgers I eat are thoroughly cooked," she explained.[1]

## When Food Makes You Sick

Food is an important part of our everyday lives. It provides the body cells with important nutrients we need to live. Sometimes, however, the food we eat can make us sick. Every year, millions of Americans get sick from something they ate. In fact, many people will have some kind of food poisoning a number of times during their lifetime.

Food poisoning is an illness caused by contaminated food or drink. Food is said to be contaminated if it has been in contact with something harmful. It may contain certain bacteria, viruses, parasites, molds, yeasts, their toxins, or toxins found in the food itself.

Most cases of food poisoning are caused by microorganisms. Under the right conditions—a warm, moist environment with plenty of food—germs can grow and multiply. Bacteria can grow quickly in food if it is left out at room temperature for too long. Some bacteria produce toxins as they grow in food. When people eat the food, the toxins may make them sick.

Food poisoning is an illness caused by contaminated food or drink. It may contain certain bacteria, viruses, parasites, molds, yeasts, their toxins, or toxins found in the food itself.

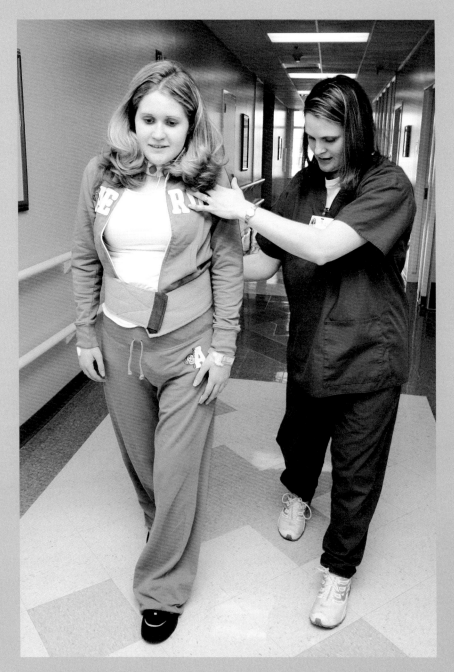

Fourteen-year-old Leah (left) gets help from a physical therapist as she recovers from botulism poisoning. The botulism came from a home-canned stew that she ate at her relative's home.

## Multiplying by Dividing

When a person eats food contaminated with disease-causing bacteria, the bacteria can multiply quickly inside the body. Each bacterium reproduces by dividing into two smaller bacteria. Each offspring grows and then divides, too. When the temperature is just right and there is plenty of food, one bacterium can divide into two bacteria every 20 to 30 minutes. A few bacteria would not be enough to make a person feel ill, but after a few hours, just one germ could multiply into millions!

Some germs make people sick after they multiply inside the body. People often don't realize that food has gone bad because many bacteria do not make food smell or look different.

Foods that are most likely to be contaminated include poultry (chicken, duck, turkey), meats (beef, pork, lamb), seafood (fish, oysters, shrimp), eggs, and dairy products (milk, cheese, yogurt). Food manufacturers use various methods to keep foods free of harmful germs or to prevent them from multiplying. Milk is pasteurized (heated briefly to a high temperature, then rapidly cooled) to kill bacteria. Deep-freezing and drying foods prevent the growth of germs. Canned foods can be kept safely for a long time because most

Uncooked meat is one food most likely to contain harmful germs. Cooking food thoroughly, to the proper temperature, kills the bacteria that could otherwise be harmful.

bacteria cannot grow and multiply without air. However, the deadliest form of food poisoning, botulism, is caused by a type of bacterium that *can* grow without air. Normally, bacteria are killed by the heat and high pressures of the canning process. If canning is not done properly, however, they can grow and multiply and produce a very deadly toxin.

People may unknowingly buy foods that do contain bacteria. Vegetables that are eaten raw, such as lettuce, may still carry bacteria from the soil in which they were grown. More bacteria may have been added by

> Foods that are most likely to be contaminated include poultry, meats, seafood, eggs, and dairy products.

people who handled them during washing and packing. Washing raw vegetables thoroughly can help get rid of most of the bacteria.

Meats and poultry sold in the supermarket may contain bacteria as well. Eggs may also be contaminated, although the risk is relatively low. The bacteria in meats and other foods that are cooked do not usually cause illness because high temperatures kill bacteria. Freezing food can keep bacteria from growing and multiplying— but it does not kill them. The bacteria will become active again once the food is thawed. Keeping food refrigerated may help to keep most bacteria from growing, but the best way to destroy the bacteria is by cooking the food thoroughly.

According to the CDC, 97 percent of all cases of food poisoning are due to poor handling of food.[2] For example, people may not wash their hands after going to the bathroom. (Bacteria are found in a person's feces.) The germs can spread to other people when those who are infected prepare a meal for their family or for people in a restaurant. Remember that Typhoid Mary spread the typhoid bacterium to a number of

# Common Bacteria That Cause Food Poisoning

| Type of Bacterium | How It Spreads | Symptoms |
|---|---|---|
| Campylobacter | Untreated drinking water; infected pets; unpasteurized milk; contaminated raw or undercooked meat, poultry, or shellfish | Diarrhea (possibly bloody), cramps, fever, headache |
| *Clostridium botulinum* (Botulism) | Contaminated canned foods or sausages | Double vision, droopy eyelids, trouble speaking, swallowing, or breathing; can be deadly if not treated |
| *Escherichia coli* O157:H7 | Contaminated drinking water, raw or under-cooked ground beef, unpasteurized milk, salad greens (lettuces) | Severe abdominal cramps, diarrhea (often bloody), nausea, vomiting, fever; may need hospitalization |
| Listeria | Untreated drinking water, unpasteurized milk and other dairy products, contaminated undercooked meat and seafood, contaminated cold cuts, raw vegetables fertilized with infected manure | *Adults:* fever, chills, muscle aches, nausea, diarrhea; *Infants:* vomiting, will not drink, breathing difficulty |
| Salmonella | Eating or touching contaminated under-cooked chicken, eggs, or beef; infected pets | Nausea, fever, stomach cramps, diarrhea, vomiting |
| Shigella | Contaminated poultry, milk and other dairy products, salad greens; often spread due to poor sanitary practices | Abdominal pain, fever, sometimes vomiting, mucus in stool |

people when she worked as a cook. She was a carrier—
she had no symptoms of the disease, but she could pass
the germ on to others.

Bacteria that normally live in the nose and throat or
on the skin may cause trouble if they contaminate food
and then multiply when
the food is left at room
temperature. CDC investi-
gators also found that 79
percent of food-poisoning
cases were due to food from restaurants, school lunch-
rooms, and other public eating places, and 21 percent
resulted from food prepared in the home.[3]

According to the CDC, 97 percent
of all cases of food poisoning are
due to poor handling of food.

## What Happens When You Get Food Poisoning?

Even if you eat contaminated food, you are not
guaranteed to get food poisoning. Whether or not you
get sick depends on a number of things: your age, how
much of the contaminated food you ate, and how
strong your immune system is. The immune system
includes various cells and chemicals that help defend
the body against germs and other foreign substances.
Normally, the immune system does a good job protecting

the body from harmful "invaders." If it didn't, you would get sick much more often.

Let's say you eat some chicken that is contaminated with salmonella bacteria. Taking just one bite can carry thousands of bacteria into your body. Once they are swallowed, the bacteria travel to the stomach, where most of them are killed by the stomach acid there. However, some bacteria sur-vive the acid bath. They are sent on to the intestines by the muscular contractions that push food through the digestive tract. In the intestines, the bac-teria find everything they need

> Whether or not you get sick depends on a number of things: your age, how much of the contaminated food you ate, and how strong your immune system is.

to grow and multiply—warmth, moisture, and plenty of food. They head toward the lining of the intestines. The bacteria invade cells on the surface and start to multiply.

Within a few hours, the infected cells in the intestinal lining start to die. Soon the bacteria spread to nearby cells and infect them, too. In less than eight hours, there may be a million salmonella bacteria roaming inside your intestines. Their population continues to grow, doubling in as little as 20 to 30 minutes.

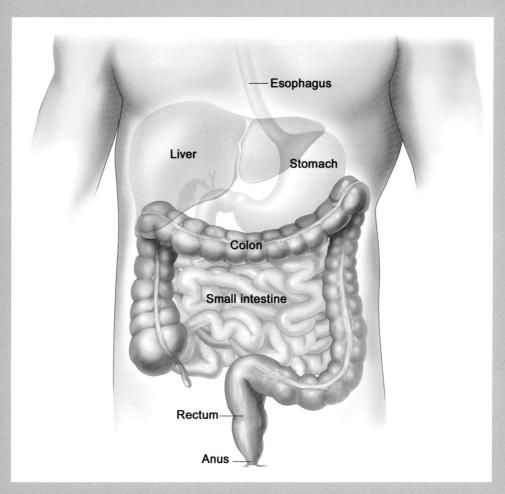

The gastrointestinal system is the part of the body affected by food poisoning. It includes the stomach and the intestines (small intestine and large intestine, or colon).

You may not realize that all this is going on, but your immune system soon finds out. When the body cells are damaged, they send out chemicals that alert the body's defenders to the danger. Some of these chemicals cause fluid to leak out of the blood vessels and into the body tissues, making them swell. The process is called inflammation. Other chemicals produced by damaged cells alert white blood cells, the body's main line of defense.

White blood cells are jelly-like blobs that can swim freely through the blood. They can also move easily through inflamed, fluid-filled tissues. Some of the white blood cells make chemical weapons called antibodies that kill germs or stop them from multiplying. Other white cells swarm over the germs and gobble them up. However, some white blood cells are killed by poisons from the salmonella bacteria they have eaten.

As the bacteria kill more and more cells, you start to feel sick. The muscles in your stomach wall start to contract (tighten) so much that it hurts. The intestines contract, too, but instead of sending the food along its usual route, they may squeeze some of it back into the stomach. Meanwhile, messages are sent along nerves from the throat and stomach to a special vomiting center in your brain. You begin to feel nauseous, "sick to

## Summer Is Peak Season

Summer is a time for picnics and barbecues with family and friends. What could be nicer than warm weather and good food? Unfortunately, those also happen to be the perfect conditions for microorganisms to multiply. In the hot summer sun, microorganisms can multiply in food really fast,  especially when the temperature is above 90°F (32°C). Since more people eat outside during the summer months than any other time of the year, it's no wonder that summertime is peak season for food poisoning.

your stomach." As the stomach contractions get stronger, the vomiting center makes the valve at the top of the stomach pop open, and you throw up. All your stomach's contents go gushing up through the esophagus and out of your mouth. This is actually your body's way of protecting you—by getting rid of the poisons.

The contractions in your small intestine also continue and get stronger. You may feel these contractions as painful cramps, but they are helping to get rid of the poison by moving partially digested food along much faster than usual. You may get a sudden urge to go to the bathroom, and when you do, your stools (body wastes) are soft or even liquid. You have diarrhea. The stools are so watery because the wastes did not spend much time in your large intestine, where excess water is normally removed. Diarrhea is not a pleasant experience, but it removes millions of bacteria from your body.

As more and more body cells are damaged, there is a buildup of chemicals being released in the body. Soon inflammation develops in the muscles, and your body aches. In the meantime, the numerous trips to the bathroom have made you lose a serious amount of water, and you become dehydrated. You feel tired, and your head starts to pound.

As the salmonella bacteria continue to spread, the immune system calls for reinforcements. More white blood cells swarm in. Some have grown into giant cells, twice the usual size. They are called macrophages, which literally means "big eaters." That is exactly what they do—they gobble up bacteria and digest them, breaking them down with powerful proteins called enzymes. Meanwhile, other white blood cells have attached bits of salmonella to their outer surface, like warriors that take trophies from defeated enemies. These cells travel through the bloodstream and help the immune system to recognize the enemy bacteria.

In the lymph nodes (clumps of immune system cells), specialized cells turn into antibody-making factories. The huge numbers of antibodies they produce can attach to the chemicals on the outside of salmonella bacteria. Some of these antibodies damage the bacteria; others make them easier for the macrophages to catch and kill. As the body's defenders are strengthened by all these reinforcements, they begin to win their battles against the invading germs. Within a few days, the numbers of bacteria have dropped substantially, and the bouts of nausea and diarrhea stop. Still, it will take a few weeks for the white blood cells to kill all of the salmonella remaining in your body. White blood cell scavengers act as a clean-up squad, gobbling up bacteria and bits of dead body cells. Finally you are back to normal.

## What Are the Symptoms?

Food poisoning can have a variety of causes, so symptoms can vary. However, many types of food poisoning do share some common symptoms: nausea, vomiting, abdominal cramps, and diarrhea. It takes time after exposure for symptoms to develop. This is called the incubation period. How long it takes depends on the type of organism or toxin that was swallowed, and how much of it survived the acid bath in the stomach. Many people think that food poisoning is

> Symptoms may develop in as little as 30 minutes after eating the contaminated food, or they may be delayed for days or even weeks.

caused by the last meal that the sick person ate, but that is not always true. Symptoms may develop in as little as 30 minutes after eating the contaminated food, or they may be delayed for days or even weeks. Often the symptoms get worse as time goes by.

Health experts say that certain groups of people have a higher risk than others of getting sick from food

Some people take antacids to help the stomach upsets that are caused by food poisoning.

poisoning, and of having more serious problems. These
high-risk groups include:

- the elderly (because their immune system
  may not be as strong as when they were younger)
- infants and young children (because their
  immune system is not yet fully developed)
- people with chronic disease (such as diabetes,
  cancer, or AIDS), whose immune system is
  weakened
- pregnant women (food poisoning leads to
  dehydration and may harm or even kill the
  unborn child)

# 4

# What Causes Food Poisoning?

I N MAY 1998, a twelve-year-old British girl, Zoe Jeffries, told her mother that she was having leg pains. Soon she developed headaches as well. Then Zoe's behavior started to change. She was having crying fits that often lasted for hours at a time. She refused to go to school, and she would not leave the house. Zoe's mother thought that her daughter—normally a popular, outgoing girl— was probably reacting to her father's death. (He had died of a heart attack a few months earlier.) Not knowing what else to do, Mrs. Jeffries took Zoe to the doctor.

The doctor thought that Zoe was depressed and prescribed antidepressants for her. The medication did not seem to help, though. In fact, Zoe was getting worse. She was fighting with her friends. Her behavior got so bad

Mad cow disease is caused by eating contaminated beef. These students in England are offered ostrich burgers instead of beef burgers, following a scare of mad cow disease.

that she could no longer go to school. She started to pull at her hair, sometimes yanking so hard that she wound up with handfuls of it. Then she was having hallucinations about "gremlins" coming into her room at night. The doctors continued to say that she was suffering from depression.

By the end of the year, Zoe was having trouble walking. She was dragging one foot and sometimes lost her balance. By early 1999, Zoe needed a wheelchair to get around. The doctors ran a number of tests, and eventually an MRI diagnosed Zoe's problem—variant Creutzfeldt-Jakob disease, or vCJD. What kind of disease was this and how did Zoe get it? Mrs. Jeffries was given pamphlets and learned that vCJD is related to mad cow disease. Zoe got sick from eating contaminated beef. She had been eating burgers and meat pies since she was two years old, as many as three times a week. After hearing this news, the Jeffries family stopped eating meat altogether.[1]

## Germs in Food

Mad cow disease—as many people call it—is a rare and unusual type of food poisoning. There are actually more than 250 known foodborne illnesses. Most types of food poisoning are caused by bacteria or other microorganisms. The illnesses caused by some of them are so common that many people are familiar with their names.

Here are some common causes of food poisoning:

Salmonella. Salmonella is a kind of bacterium that can cause several illnesses. *Salmonella typhi* causes typhoid fever. Other types of salmonella cause a type of food poisoning called salmonellosis. Salmonella poisoning is one of the most common causes of foodborne illness. Every year, about 40,000 cases of salmonella infections are reported in the United States. However, the CDC believes that the actual number could be more than thirty times that amount because many of them are so mild that they go undiagnosed.[2]

Salmonella has been found mostly in raw and undercooked eggs, undercooked and raw meat, and milk products. Bacteria from these foods can settle in the small intestine and multiply. They produce a toxin that can damage or kill body cells. When enough cells are harmed (usually within twelve to seventy-two hours after exposure), symptoms start to develop. They may include fever, diarrhea, stomach cramps, nausea, and vomiting. Symptoms usually go away on their own within four to seven days. The illness may become much more serious for people in high-risk groups. In such people the bacteria may spread to other parts of the body and damage important organs, which can result in death. An estimated 600 people die from salmonellosis in the United States each year.[3]

Salmonella can be killed by high temperatures. That is why it is very important to cook eggs, poultry, and meat completely, to kill any salmonella bacteria they may contain. And people should always wash their

## Poison Pets?

Many people like to keep reptiles and amphibians as pets. What they may not realize is that these animals may carry salmonella, the bacterium that is typically linked with food poisoning. Salmonella can be found in the animal's feces and can spread to people when the pet is handled. People should always wash their hands after handling a reptile or amphibian.

hands after handling eggs, raw meat, or poultry. Otherwise, the bacteria could get into their body if they touch their eyes, nose, or mouth.

Campylobacter. Although salmonella is the best-known cause of food poisoning, campylobacter is actually the most common cause of foodborne illness. Campylobacter is a bacterium that causes an illness called campylobacteriosis. It is estimated that 2.4 million Americans are affected by this germ each year.[4]

Campylobacter has been found in raw or under-cooked meat and poultry, unpasteurized milk, untreated drinking water, and raw or undercooked shellfish. Within two to five days after exposure, the infected person may develop diarrhea, cramping, stomach pain, and fever. Diarrhea may become bloody. The illness usually goes away on its own within a week. However, people in high-risk groups may develop complications, such as Guillain-Barre syndrome, a rare condition that can cause paralysis. Although campylobacter infections do not usually lead to death, the CDC estimates that 124 Americans die from this illness each year.[5]

Listeria. Listeria is a bacterium that causes an infection called listeriosis. This illness has recently been discovered to be a serious health problem in the United States. It affects mainly pregnant women, newborns, and adults with weakened immune systems. While it may not be as well known as some other foodborne illnesses, listeriosis is much more deadly. The CDC estimates about 2,500 people are infected by listeria in the United States each year. Of these people, 500 die.[6]

Listeria is commonly found in plants, animals, water, and soil. The bacteria can be spread to people through untreated water, unpasteurized milk and dairy products, raw meat and seafood, and vegetables grown in contaminated soil or fertilized with infected manure. Listeria can be killed by high temperatures, but some

ready-to-eat foods, such as cold cuts, may become contaminated during packaging, after they have already
been cooked.

When listeria invades the human body, it may take
two to thirty days for symptoms to develop. Adults
infected with listeria may develop a fever, chills, nausea,
and diarrhea. An infant may throw up, refuse to drink,
or have trouble breathing. Serious complications may
occur, such as blood poisoning or meningitis
(inflammation of the coverings of the brain). The

Listeria can be found in cold cuts.

infection may even kill a pregnant woman's unborn child. These complications can be avoided if the illness is caught early enough and treated with medicine.

E. coli O157:H7. There are hundreds of strains of *E. coli* bacteria, most of which are harmless. But this particular strain—*E. coli* O157:H7— *is* harmful. (The O157:H7 part of the name allows scientists to distinguish it from other strains.) It produces a powerful toxin that can

## Spinach Scare

In September 2006, grocery stores in more than twenty states had to pull bags of prepackaged spinach off the shelves. Outbreaks of food poisoning affecting more than one hundred people— including at least one death—had been traced to fresh spinach grown on a farm in California. The illness was caused by *E. coli* O157:H7 infections. Health officials believe that the spinach could have become contaminated either in the field or during packaging. The bacteria may also have gotten into the water used to irrigate the crops. Wild pigs that had broken through the fences around the spinach field may have carried in the bacteria. The pigs tested positive for the same *E. coli* strain that caused the outbreak. This was the twentieth outbreak of food poisoning linked to fresh spinach or lettuce since 1995.[9]

make people extremely sick. Each year, *E. coli* O157:H7 affects about 73,000 people in the United States. About 61 people die from the infection.[7]

*E. coli* O157:H7 has been found in raw or undercooked ground beef, salami, unpasteurized milk and juice, sprouts, salad greens, and untreated water. People can also become infected by swimming in water contaminated with animal or human waste. Within three to four days after exposure, the infected person may develop severe stomach cramps, followed by diarrhea that often turns bloody. Other symptoms may include nausea, vomiting, and a low-grade fever. In most cases, the illness goes away on its own in five to ten days. In high-risk groups, especially in children under five and the elderly, the illness can lead to hemolytic uremic syndrome (HUS), a condition that can result in kidney failure. This complication occurs in about 2 to 7 percent of *E. coli* infections.[8]

Shigella. Shigella is a kind of bacterium that causes an illness called shigellosis. About 18,000 cases are reported in the United States every year. However, the actual number may be twenty times that amount because milder cases usually are not diagnosed or reported.[10] Shigella is typically spread by people who do not wash their hands after going to the bathroom and then serve food to others. (Like many other foodborne bacteria, shigella is found in the feces of infected people.) Outbreaks often occur in crowded places, such as day-care centers and nursing homes. Shigellosis is much more common in developing countries, where conditions are often crowded and not particularly clean.

Shigella has been found in raw or undercooked poultry, unpasteurized milk and dairy products, and salad greens. If a person does become infected, symptoms will start to develop within a day or two after eating the contaminated food. Symptoms may include stomach cramps, fever, and diarrhea, which often turns bloody. The illness goes away on its own within five to seven days. For some people, especially young children and the elderly, severe diarrhea may lead to dehydration and a trip to the hospital may be necessary.

Botulism. Botulism is a rare but deadly illness. It is caused by a powerful toxin produced by the bacterium *Clostridium botulinum.* There are actually three main kinds of botulism: foodborne, infant, and wound. Foodborne botulism accounts for only 25 percent of the estimated 110 cases of botulism reported in the United State each year. Infant botulism makes up the majority—

about 72 percent—of the reported cases. The remaining cases are wound botulism.[11]

Botulinum bacteria are commonly found in soil and dust. Wound botulism occurs when the bacteria enter a cut or wound and then release their poison into the body.

Infant botulism may develop when babies put dirty items containing botulinum bacteria into their mouths. The bacteria get into their bodies, multiply in their intestines, and release their toxin. Some cases of infant botulism are actually a type of foodborne illness. They are caused by eating honey, which sometimes contains botulinum bacteria. Researchers suggest that the bees that make the honey may have picked up the bacteria from the environment. (Health experts advise that honey should not be given babies under one year old.)

Foodborne botulism is often caused by eating foods that have been canned or preserved at home. The bacteria may have been picked up from the soil in which the fruit or vegetables were grown, or they were introduced during handling. Ordinary boiling will kill most germs, but botulinum bacteria can survive by changing into a special form, called a spore. Bacterial spores are covered by a thick, tough overcoat and just rest until conditions are better for growth. Usually the combination of high temperature and high pressure during the canning process *does* kill botulinum bacteria.

Botulism from commercial canned foods is extremely rare. In home canning, however, the temperature and pressure may not be high enough to kill all the spores. The few spores that survive become active again in the sealed canned foods, multiplying and producing their toxin. Botulinum bacteria are most likely to grow in foods with a low acid level, such as asparagus, green beans, beets, and corn. (Tomatoes and pickles are usually

## A Helpful Poison?

Botulinum toxin is one of the deadliest of all poisons, but doctors have found a use for it. They use this toxin, in a purified form called BOTOX, to safely treat various muscle problems, such as constant twitching in an eyelid, arm, or leg. Injecting a tiny amount of BOTOX blocks the incoming messages from the nerves to the muscles and stops the twitching. When injected into the muscles of the face, BOTOX can smooth out wrinkles—but the effects last only a few months, and then another injection is needed. More and more people are using BOTOX to get rid of their wrinkles so that they can stay young-looking. BOTOX has also been approved as a treatment for excessive sweating.

too acidic for the bacteria to grow.) To be safe, home-canned foods should be boiled for at least ten minutes before eating. This will destroy toxins produced by any bacteria that survived.

When a person eats food contaminated with the botulinum bacteria, it may take eighteen to thirty-six hours for symptoms to develop. Botulinum toxin targets the nervous system, which can lead to serious problems. Symptoms may include blurred or double vision, muscle weakness, slurred speech, droopy eyelids, and difficulty swallowing. If the illness is not treated, it can lead to paralysis in the arms, legs, trunk, and even breathing muscles. When the breathing muscles are affected, botulism may result in death. Protect yourself by throwing out any bulging or swollen cans in your home. Bulging, which may be a sign of contamination, is due to a buildup of gas produced by the growing bacteria.

Noroviruses. The germs most commonly involved in food poisoning are noroviruses (also called Norwalk-like viruses). Chances are that people who say they have the "stomach flu" are probably infected with these viruses. The CDC estimates that noroviruses cause about 23 million cases of food poisoning each year.[12] Like many food-poisoning bacteria, noroviruses are found in the

Noroviruses are the most common germs involved in food poisoning. They spread quickly in crowded areas such as day-care centers and cruise ships.

vomit and stool of infected people. The viruses can spread very easily in a number of ways: by consuming food or drink contaminated with the norovirus; by touching contaminated objects, such as a doorknob, and then touching one's mouth, or through direct contact with the infected person or sharing his or her food or utensils.

Noroviruses can spread very quickly in crowded places, such as day-care centers, nursing homes, and cruise ships. Symptoms start to develop within twenty-four to forty-eight hours after exposure. They may include a lot of vomiting, diarrhea along with stomach cramps, and nausea. Some people may also develop a low-grade fever, chills, headache, muscle aches, and a general feeling of tiredness.

Although noroviruses can make a person really miserable, most people feel better within one to two days. However, people in high-risk groups may become seriously dehydrated and should seek medical attention.

Mad cow disease. Although this foodborne illness has been in the news a lot, mad cow disease is actually very rare. It is caused by defective proteins, called prions, which are found in the brain tissue of infected cattle. Prions literally eat away at the brain, leaving spongelike holes. It can take as long as ten years for symptoms to develop. The cow becomes aggressive and has trouble walking. Eventually, it dies.

If people eat meat from infected cattle, they may develop the human form of mad cow disease, known as variant Creutzfeldt-Jakob disease (vCJD). Signs and symptoms of vCJD may include memory loss, mood changes, dizziness, difficulty walking, muscle spasms, loss of speech, and blindness.

No way to kill prions has yet been discovered. Prions survive in conditions that would kill most bacteria and viruses, including extreme heat, ultraviolet light and other radiation, and disinfectants. Animals and people infected with prions are likely to die.

Mad cow disease first appeared in dairy cows in Great Britain in the mid-1980s. Thousands of cows were affected. The disease spread rapidly through infected feed. Farmers commonly included animal parts in cattle feed to provide extra protein for growing. Some of these parts were infected with prions. News of this "mad cow disease" stirred up panic in people all over Britain.

The first human case of infection with the prions of mad cow disease was diagnosed in 1994. As more human cases were reported, various countries took legal action to prevent it from spreading. Starting in March 1996, British beef could no longer be exported to other countries. In 1997, the use of animal parts in cattle feed was officially banned. Even though the source was eliminated, many cattle were already infected and would not show symptoms for many years. In 2000, health officials required testing for prions throughout Europe

A farmer in England worries about the effect of mad cow disease on his family farming business.

in efforts to keep the infected cattle out of the food supply.

By April 2005, more than 184,000 cases of mad cow disease had occurred in cattle in Great Britain alone.[13] The risk of infecting humans is very low, however. By November 2006, worldwide, a total of 200 cases of mad cow disease in humans (vCJD) had been confirmed by laboratory tests. Most of them (164) occurred in Great Britain. Many Americans worry about mad cow disease and the safety of the beef in the United States. However, as of November 2006 there had been only three cases of vCJD in the United States. Two of them were believed to have been infected in Great Britain, and the other was a recent immigrant from Saudi Arabia.[14]

## Poisons in Food

Some foods contain their own natural poisons and may be harmful if you eat them. Certain fungi, for example, contain poisons that can make people sick. Mushrooms, molds, mildew, and yeast are all fungi. There are actually thousands of different kinds of mushrooms in North America, but only about a hundred of them are poisonous. The mushrooms sold in stores are not harmful, and many people love to eat them. Just be sure not to pick any wild mushrooms. It is not easy to identify whether a mushroom is poisonous or not, so it is best to leave them alone.

You may have seen that gray, fuzzy-looking stuff that grows on foods left in the refrigerator too long. That's mold, and like mushrooms, it is a type of fungus. If you look at mold under a microscope, it will look like skinny mushrooms. Mold forms spores, which can float through the air and land on food, where they can grow and reproduce if the conditions are right. Mold grows best in warm and moist conditions. But unlike most

These researchers are testing shellfish for toxins. Shellfish make toxins that can cause food poisoning.

bacteria, mold and other fungi can live in very hot or very cold environments. That is why refrigerating food may keep bacteria from growing, but it won't keep mold from growing on fruits and vegetables, or in a jar of spaghetti sauce. Cooking moldy food at high temperatures will not kill the mold spores.

You might get sick from eating a slice of moldy bread or a piece of moldy cheese, but these kinds of molds usually do not cause serious harm. Some molds, however, produce poisonous substances called mycotoxins. These molds are found mainly in grains and nuts, although they may also grow on celery, grape juice, apples, and other produce. Probably the best known and most carefully studied mycotoxin is aflatoxin. This is a cancer-causing poison found in certain molds that grow mainly in stored crops, especially peanuts and corn. Aflatoxin has been linked to a number of diseases in livestock, domestic animals, and humans all over the world.

Clams, oysters, and other shellfish may become contaminated with poisons from the water creatures on which they feed. Much of their diet includes algae and other microscopic organisms (called plankton) that live in the surface waters. At certain times of the year, some of the plankton organisms, such as red algae, have a sudden population explosion, multiplying in such huge numbers that they stain the water red. (These times are known as red tides.) Plankton can produce poisonous chemicals that become concentrated in the bodies of animals that feed on them, especially during red tides. These days, shellfish is monitored and tested regularly, so the risk of eating this kind of contaminated shellfish is very low. However, eating raw shellfish can be risky because they may carry disease-causing viruses and parasites. They may pick up hepatitis A virus, for example, if the waters in which they grow are contaminated by sewage.

Most fruits and vegetables are sprayed with pesticides, chemicals that farmers use to get rid of insects and other pests. Fruits and vegetables should be washed before eating them so that these chemicals won't get into your body. Eating just one apple without washing it will not harm you. It will probably contain only traces of pesticides. However, if you never wash the foods you

## Poisonous Puffer

The puffer, also called the blowfish, is one of the most poisonous sea creatures, but some people like to eat it. This fish is famous for blowing itself up like a balloon when it is frightened. It carries a deadly poison in certain parts of its body. In Japan, specially trained cooks prepare puffers for eating by taking out the liver and other poisonous parts. The rest is safe to eat. The fish *must* be prepared properly, though, or it could have deadly results.

eat, poisons may build up in your body. It may take years, but eventually they could damage important organs, like the brain, heart, and liver.

The Environmental Protection Agency (EPA) sets limits for the amounts of pesticides and other chemicals that may remain in foods. These "residues" are so small that they are not considered harmful. The Food and Drug Administration (FDA) and the U.S. Department of Agriculture (USDA) check foods to make sure that they do not contain residues above the legal limits. State agencies also test foods produced locally. Moreover, chemical companies are developing pesticides that are less toxic to humans.

# 5

# Detection and Treatment

**F**OR TWENTY-FIVE YEARS, Patricia Griffin had worked as a food writer for the foodborne disease branch of the CDC. She had plenty of experience in interviewing victims of foodborne illnesses and parents whose children had died from them. In the summer of 2005, however, Patricia had a frightening firsthand experience with foodborne illness when her nine-year-old daughter, Anna, developed a bad case of salmonella poisoning.

During a family vacation in Florida, Anna Griffin suddenly developed severe stomach pains and bouts of diarrhea that sent her dashing to the bathroom. Feeling absolutely miserable, she told her mom it was like "having my butt on full blast."[1] When Anna became weaker and dehydrated, her parents took her to the hospital.

After hearing about Anna's symptoms, a doctor in the emergency room (ER) suspected appendicitis and ordered a battery of tests, including a sonogram, an X-ray, and a CT scan. Patricia, however, believed that her daughter might have a foodborne illnesses. She suggested that the doctor take a stool culture, which is the standard diagnostic test for foodborne illness.

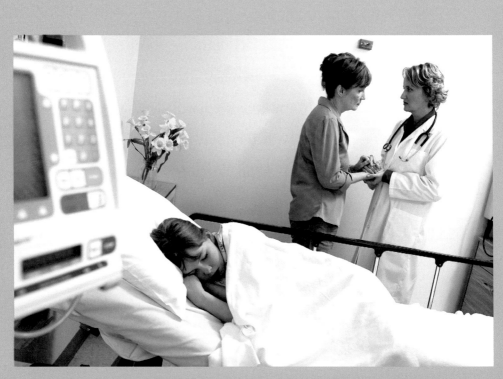

When food poisoning is serious, a trip to the hospital may be necessary.

The doctor ignored her request. Patricia was annoyed. She agreed that it was a good idea to rule out appendicitis, but food poisoning seemed like another obvious possibility.

Another doctor came on duty that night, and Patricia asked her to take a stool sample. The doctor agreed, although she thought Anna probably had a gastrointestinal virus—like five other kids who had been treated in the ER that night. When the test results finally came back a few days later, they showed that Anna had salmonellosis. Patricia tried to piece together what Anna had eaten during their vacation, and where she had eaten it. Eventually, she figured out that the illness was probably caused by a batch of undercooked chicken tenders Anna had eaten at a restaurant. Patricia remembered that Anna had started having stomach problems about ten hours after eating that meal. Anna recalled that some of the chicken tenders had been cold and hard.

Patricia later asked an ER doctor why they don't take stool cultures anymore. She was told that the results are not very helpful since they usually do not come back for a couple of days. In the case of food poisoning, a positive test result does not have any effect on the treatment. (In fact, for many cases there is no specific treatment except to keep the patient hydrated.) Doctors generally focus on treating their individual patients. What is the point of running tests that will not help the patients get well?

Patricia saw things differently. As a worker for the CDC, she knew how important it was to identify food-borne illnesses. That way health agencies could keep track of outbreaks and protect people from future contaminations.

In the meantime, Anna was prescribed the typical treatment for food poisoning: the BRAT diet. *BRAT* stands for *b*ananas, *r*ice, *a*pplesauce, and *t*oast, which are foods that are easy on the stomach and help the digestive system get back to normal. After two weeks of missing school, Anna was feeling like her old self again. The experience has not made her nervous about eating out at restaurants, but she and her mother are careful to order meats that are "fully cooked."[2]

## Is It Food Poisoning?

Every year, millions of people get food poisoning, but most of them do not go to the doctor. Usually they feel better within a day or two, so these cases go unreported.

Many people do not even realize that the illness they have is food poisoning. The symptoms are often confused with those of a common viral infection. In fact, people who describe symptoms of nausea, vomiting, or diarrhea tend to say that they have the "stomach flu" or a "stomach virus." Medical experts do not like the term *stomach flu* because they believe it causes confusion about what flu (influenza) really is. The influenza virus targets the respiratory system—the breathing passages and lungs. The viruses that attack the gastrointestinal system—the stomach and intestines—are quite different. They cause vomiting and diarrhea, which are *not* symptoms of the flu.

Every year, millions of people get food poisoning, but most of them do not go to the doctor. Usually they feel better within a day or two, so these cases go unreported.

Diagnosing food poisoning can take some detective work. The doctor must ask some key questions that will give clues to the patient's illness: What are your symptoms? When did you first get sick? What have you eaten in the last few days? Did you eat the meals at home or at a restaurant? Has anyone else in your family gotten sick? After gathering all the clues, the doctor may make an initial diagnosis of food poisoning. Tests can confirm the diagnosis. However, treatment is usually started right away, since it takes a couple of days for the test results to come back—and treatment is basically the same in most cases. Early treatment is especially important for botulism, which can have devastating

## Foods the Body Can't Handle

What might look like food poisoning could actually be an allergy. Many people have problems when they eat certain foods because they have an allergy to them. An allergy causes a person's body to overreact to a substance that does not normally bother most people. If someone has an allergy to strawberries, for example, eating a couple of them may give this person a bad stomachache or produce a skin rash. Allergies to peanuts may cause breathing difficulty and other serious—and even life-threatening—reactions.

Some people can't drink milk or eat other dairy products. Their bodies have a problem digesting these foods properly. These people have a condition called lactose intolerance. Milk contains lactose, which is a milk sugar. Lactose-intolerant people don't have an enzyme called lactase, which is needed to digest milk products. When they drink milk or eat cheese or ice cream, they may get a stomachache, gas, or diarrhea.

Doctors are like disease detectives, asking many questions to determine the cause of a case of food poisoning.

effects on the patient and can lead to death if left untreated.

A stool culture is the standard diagnostic test for food poisoning. The patient provides a stool sample, which is then cultured—grown in a laboratory under conditions that allow bacteria to multiply. When enough bacteria have grown, the technician can identify the type of organisms that are causing the illness. Other diagnostic tests can be performed to isolate the bacteria from vomit, blood, or any leftover contaminated food.

In some very rare cases, doctors may do further testing on patients whose symptoms do not seem to be going away. For example, a sigmoidoscopy is a test that involves a long, thin, hollow tube used to look at the inside of a patient's large intestine to find the source of bleeding or infection.

## When to See the Doctor

Most cases of food poisoning are not serious, and symptoms often go away on their own. However, some people, especially those in high-risk groups, may develop more serious problems that need immediate medical attention. People should seek medical help if they have any of the following symptoms:

- High fever (temperature over 101.5°F, or 38.6°C)
- Blood in stools or vomit
- Severe stomach pains
- Signs of dehydration, such as dry mouth, decreased urine, sunken eyes, dizziness
- Diarrhea that lasts more than three days (which can lead to dehydration)
- Ongoing vomiting that prevents keeping liquids down (which can lead to dehydration)

## How to Treat Food Poisoning

When it comes to the treatment of food poisoning, there is one main focus: to replace the fluids and electrolytes lost through vomiting and diarrhea. Electrolytes are salts and minerals that the body needs to stay healthy. A loss of fluids can lead to dehydration. Your body is two-thirds water, so when you become dehydrated, the body cannot function properly. Patients should drink plenty of fluids, especially mixtures for replacing electrolytes, such as Pedialyte® beverages. Sports drinks, such as Gatorade® brand, are not as

It is very important to drink fluids after being sick with food poisoning.

effective in replacing these lost electrolytes, and are not usually recommended as treatment for diarrheal illness. Taking antidiarrheal medicines, such as Pepto-Bismol® tablets or liquid, can help prevent dehydration.

During times of vomiting and diarrhea, people with food poisoning should try not to eat any solid food. They do need to keep hydrated, though, by drinking small amounts of clear liquids, such as water or ginger ale, throughout the day. Once vomiting and diarrhea have stopped, health experts recommend the BRAT diet for two to three days. Certain foods should be avoided at least for the first few days. They include milk and other dairy products, spicy foods, greasy fried foods, and raw fruits and vegetables.

Doctors do not usually prescribe antibiotics to treat food poisoning. Antibiotics are medicines that kill bacteria. They do not work for illnesses caused by viruses. Some severe cases of bacterial food poisoning can be treated with antibiotics. But these drugs are not usually given to people with mild cases. Medical experts worry that antibiotics are used too often. When bacteria are exposed to an antibiotic, most of them are killed, but some may survive and multiply. These drug-resistant bacteria, which can't be killed by the usual doses of the antibiotic, may be passed on to other people. The more an antibiotic is used, the more likely that drug-resistant bacteria will appear and spread. Then even very high doses of the antibiotic will not work against the disease. The bacteria may become resistant to other drugs, as well.

Botulism is treated differently from other types of bacterial food poisoning. Patients are given an antitoxin, a substance that stops the toxin (released by the bacteria) from causing further damage. The antitoxin should be given soon after symptoms first appear, while most of the toxin is circulating in the body and before it bonds to nerve endings. The doctor may also try to remove any remaining contaminated food that is still in the body by giving the patient either a substance that causes vomiting or an enema that works to loosen stools, forcing the person to go to the bathroom. Patients whose breathing muscles have already been damaged may need to be put on ventilators (breathing machines).

# 6

# Food Safety

I T WAS THE END OF THE SEMESTER, and Pat
Gallagher, a twenty-one-year-old college student,
had the dreaded job of cleaning out his refrigerator
before the holidays. It was a mess. Things were tossed on
top of one another. The stink of some of the leftover
food almost blew Pat away. Some of the strangest-look-
ing things were stuffed at the back of the refrigerator.
Pat had trouble figuring out what one item, wrapped in
a plastic bag, might have been. The contents looked
somewhat like hot dog rolls, but they had changed to a
really weird-looking blue color. They must have been in
the refrigerator for months, Pat realized. Now they were
covered with fuzzy mold.

Pat admits that he often saves leftovers, even though
he knows he probably won't eat them. "By the third

week, you know it's there, but you never get around to it," he says.[1]

Pat isn't alone. Many people keep leftovers in the refrigerator, hoping to eat them in the next day or two. Too often, though, these leftovers are "forgotten." They may get pushed to the back of the refrigerator and spend the next several months, or even years, there! When food sits too long, even in the refrigerator, it will go bad. Sometimes the food doesn't look or smell bad, but that doesn't mean that it is good to eat. If you can't remember when you had last eaten it, it is a good idea to throw it out.

Anyone can become a victim of food poisoning, but there are many things you can do to reduce your risk. In this chapter, we will discuss some very important rules of food safety that will help you avoid getting sick from the food you eat.

## Buying Food

The first step to keeping your food safe starts in the supermarket. To keep foods fresh, refrigerated items, such as meats, dairy, eggs, and fish, should be the last items put into the shopping cart. Do not buy canned foods that are bulging or dented, or jars that are cracked or have loose or bulging lids. Eggs should also be checked to make sure that they are not cracked. Do not buy unpasteurized milk products, ciders, or juices. Be careful not to buy fruit with bruised or broken skin. Bacteria can enter openings in the skin and contaminate the fruit.

When you are buying meat, poultry, fish, or dairy products, check the label. It should have an "expiration" or a "sell by" or "best if used by" date. If the current date is past the date on the label, don't buy the food. Even if

## Is "Organic" the Answer?

Foods labeled Organic have been grown without the use of pesticides or chemical fertilizers. Some people believe that these foods are worth the higher prices they cost because they do not contain added chemicals that might be toxic. While avoiding these poisons might be a good idea, organic foods can still contain toxins. The cattle manure that organic farmers use as fertilizer can be a source of *E. coli* and other intestinal bacteria. Moreover, organic foods are just as likely as those grown the conventional way to become contaminated with bacteria or viruses during picking, packing, and preparation.

the expiration date is still in the future, do not buy anything that smells bad or looks strange.

Packages of meat, fish, or poultry often leak juices. When grocery bags are being packed, bag these items separately from lettuce or other foods that will not be cooked before eating. Do not place bags with meat, poultry, or fish on top of foods or paper products. And watch for leaks when placing foods in the refrigerator. Wipe up any spills with paper towels and disinfectant solution.

## Keep Foods Refrigerated

In the grocery store, refrigerated items are the last items to buy. At home, they should be the first items put away—in the refrigerator or freezer. Remember, bacteria multiply in warmer temperatures. Perishable foods—foods that spoil—should never be left out at room temperature for more than two hours. Keeping these foods in the refrigerator or freezer can help to stop bacteria from growing. Health experts say that a thermostat should be used to make sure the temperatures are cool enough: the refrigerator should be set to 40°F (about 4°C) or below, and the freezer should be set to 0°F (−18°C). Refrigerators should never be overcrowded with food. Air needs to circulate to keep the food chilled. Freezers, on the other hand, hold their cold best when they are mostly filled with frozen foods. However, the air vents in the freezer should not be blocked.

Raw meat, poultry, and fish should be put in the freezer right away, unless these foods are going to be cooked within the next two days. Wash these items (except for ground meat) before wrapping them for freezing. They should be wrapped in heavy-duty plastic

Cold food needs to be kept cold. It is a good idea to buy refrigerated items last, right before you check out at the grocery store. Make sure you go straight home and refrigerate the food immediately.

wrap, freezer paper, or aluminum foil and sealed tightly so that they will last longer in the freezer.

Food should never be thawed at room temperature. The surface of the food will thaw long before the center, allowing time for bacteria to multiply. Food can be thawed in the refrigerator overnight. For a quicker thaw, place the food under cold running water, or defrost it in the microwave.

## Cooking Food

Cooking food thoroughly—to the proper internal temperature—can kill harmful bacteria that cause foodborne illnesses. The *internal* temperature is the temperature of the food, not that of the oven. A meat thermometer should be used to make sure food is being cooked to the right temperature. Beef roasts and steaks should be cooked to at least 145°F (63°C), ground beef to 160°F (71°C), and poultry to 180°F (82°C). Be sure to wash the meat thermometer after using it to avoid spreading germs from one food to another.

Do you like your steak or roast beef rare or well done? Rare meats are pink in the center, which means that the center part is not completely cooked. Are they safe to eat? Actually, they are, because contamination most often occurs on the surface of a piece of beef. The surface of rare steaks or roasts *is* cooked thoroughly, and so any bacteria on them have been killed. (When grilling steaks or chops on a barbecue, use tongs to handle them. Poking a fork or knife into a raw steak could push surface bacteria into the center.)

## How Hot Is the Stuffing?

What would a Thanksgiving dinner be without a juicy roast turkey, brown and crispy on the outside and stuffed with a mixture of bread, eggs, celery, and spices? If the turkey is not cooked long enough, though, it can lead to a stomachache that is not just due to overeating. The inside of the turkey, where the stuffing was packed, may have been contaminated, and the raw eggs might have contributed bacteria, too. If the temperature inside did not get high enough while the turkey was cooking, bacteria might have remained in the stuffing. While the turkey was sitting at room temperature, bacteria in the stuffing might have multiplied. A meat thermometer can help determine when the stuffing is safely cooked. The little pop-up thermometer that comes in the turkey just tells you when the meat is hot enough—it does not check the stuffing. The temperature of the stuffing should be measured separately, to be sure it has been cooked to 180°F (82°C).

Rare hamburgers are *not* safe to eat, however. During grinding, the surface of the pieces of meat is mixed with the center parts. Therefore, any pink parts in the center of a burger may contain live bacteria that could make you sick.

Raw fish and shellfish can be contaminated during handling, and they may also carry bacteria and parasites picked up from the environment. Eating sushi (which is made from pieces of raw fish) can be risky. Marinating the fish with spices and lime juice does not kill the bacteria or parasites. Cooking will make fish safe to eat, but it must be cooked thoroughly. Well-cooked fish loses its shiny appearance and breaks up easily into flakes when poked with a fork.

A microwave oven does not get hot while it is working, but it heats up food very quickly. However, there may be "cold spots" in the food, where bacteria can survive. To thoroughly kill bacteria, turn the dish and stir the contents occasionally so that the food is cooked evenly. Microwave ovens sold today usually have a turntable that rotates the food automatically while it is heating or cooking.

Eggs should be cooked until the yolks and whites are firm, not runny. (Remember, eggs may carry

Rare hamburgers are not safe to eat. Make sure hamburgers are not pink inside and are cooked to an internal temperature of 180°F.

salmonella bacteria.) Do not eat foods that contain raw eggs, such as cookie dough and eggnog. Sauces, soups, and gravies should be heated to a boil. Leftovers should be reheated thoroughly to at least 165°F (74°C).

## Cleaning Up

If you walk into a restaurant bathroom, you will probably notice a sign reminding workers to wash their hands. This rule is very important, especially for cooks and servers, who could easily spread their germs to other people's food. Washing hands with warm, soapy water will get rid of harmful bacteria that might be on them. But hands need to be washed for more than a couple of seconds. Health experts say that to send the bacteria down the drain you should wash your hands for at least 20 seconds.

Washing hands is a good rule to follow at home, as well. People should always wash their hands after playing with pets, changing diapers, and, of course, going to the bathroom. Germs can spread easily, especially in a kitchen. Bacteria can spread to your hands, countertops, utensils, cutting boards, and then to other foods, making them more likely to cause illness. Health experts call this *cross-contamination.*

Wash your hands thoroughly with soap and warm water before preparing food or eating. Also, wash your hands after you handle raw meat and eggs. Always wash your hands after using the bathroom.

It is important to wash hands, utensils, and surfaces thoroughly before and after handling food.

Fruits and vegetables that will be eaten raw should be washed first. Even oranges, melons, and other fruits whose outer covering is not eaten need to be washed, because a knife or fingers might carry bacteria from the surface into the fruit during preparation.

Do not use the same cutting board for raw vegetables that was used for raw meats. Germs can spread from one food to another when raw meat is cut

Never use the same cutting board or knife for raw vegetables and lettuce if you have already used it for raw meats. The bacteria from the meat will contaminate the raw vegetables. Since the vegetables will not be cooked, the bacteria will not be killed.

on a cutting board, and then the unwashed cutting board is used to chop raw vegetables. If possible, use two separate cutting boards, one for meats and one for vegetables. Always wash cutting boards thoroughly in hot water between uses. Use a paper towel to clean up meat juices, and then throw the towel away. This is a better choice than a sponge that is often used to wipe the kitchen sink and counters. Lots of germs can grow on a kitchen sponge; it is damp and contains bits of food on which bacteria can feed. To keep a sponge from

## The Fabulous Four

**CLEAN**
Wash hands
and surfaces
often.

**SEPARATE**
Don't cross-contaminate.

**CHILL**
Refrigerate promptly.

**COOK**
Cook to proper
temperatures.

Remember these four basic rules of food safety:

- *Clean.* Wash hands, utensils, and surfaces before and after handling food, and always wash hands after going to the bathroom. Wash fruits and vegetables thoroughly to remove pesticides, dirt, and bacteria before eating.
- *Separate.* Avoid cross-contamination by keeping raw meats, poultry, and seafood separate from salads and other ready-to-eat foods.
- *Cook.* Cook meats, poultry, fish, and eggs thoroughly. Use a meat thermometer to check the internal temperature of the foods.
- *Chill.* Refrigerate or freeze perishables, prepared foods, and leftovers within two hours. Do not thaw food at room temperature. Instead, use the refrigerator, cold running water, or a microwave oven. Do not crowd the refrigerator with food. Air needs to circulate to cool food properly.

> Always wash cutting boards thoroughly in hot water between uses. Use a paper towel to clean up meat juices, and then throw the towel away.

getting smelly, wash it thoroughly with a disinfectant solution that kills bacteria and fungi. Once it gets smelly, throw it out. A dishcloth may be used to clean countertops, but it can get just as dirty as a sponge. Dishcloths should be hung to dry between uses, and they should be washed frequently in the washing machine.

Is your refrigerator packed with food? Chances are some of that food has been in there for too long. Experts say that people should clean out their refrigerators once a week. If the milk smells a little funny, or you notice mold growing on the leftovers, don't try it to see if it tastes okay. (You will not get food poisoning from eating a moldy piece of cheese, but it probably won't taste very good. You may be able to save some of the cheese by cutting off the moldy part. Cheese is one of the few foods for which this practice is safe.) Even if food looks and smells okay, it may not be safe to eat. If it is past its expiration date, throw it out. The same is true for a container of leftovers that has been in there for over four or five days. When it comes to cleaning out the refrigerator, just remember: *When in doubt, throw it out!*

### Food Irradiation

The idea of irradiated food scares a lot of people. When they hear the word *radiation,* they think of cancer and other harmful effects. Actually, though, radiation is all around us. A microwave oven uses radiation to cook foods. If you break your arm, the doctor can use an X-ray machine to send radiation through your arm to take a picture of the bones inside. The air is filled with radio waves that radios and TV sets can turn into sounds and pictures. Even sunshine contains radiation—not only light but also heat and ultraviolet (UV) rays.

Radiation is energy carried in the form of rays or tiny particles too small to see without a very powerful

## Space Food

Astronauts have been eating irradiated foods since the 1970s. Crews of the space shuttle eat irradiated meat products such as beefsteak and sliced turkey. Steaks, for example, are cooked, packaged in individual pouches, and then irradiated. The treated steaks do not spoil during the spaceflight, even though it may be months before they are eaten. (There are no refrigerators on the spacecraft.)

microscope. Most of the radiation in our world is present in small amounts or does not contain enough energy to do any harm. Many repeated exposures to radiation can be dangerous, though: too much sun or having too many X-rays, for example.

When foods are irradiated, they are treated with high-energy gamma rays, X-rays, or electrons. The radiation kills bacteria and other microorganisms. Irradiation can also help to control insects and parasites and prevent spoilage. After the treatment, no radiation remains in the food. Therefore, eating irradiated food will not expose you to "harmful radiation." Irradiation may change some of the food chemicals, however, resulting in changes in taste and a loss of small amounts of nutrients. (Cooking foods also changes their taste and destroys some of the nutrients.)

The Food and Drug Administration (FDA) and the U.S. Department of Agriculture have approved the use of irradiation for a variety of foods, including spices, fruits, vegetables, raw meats, and poultry. Ready-to-eat foods, such as deli meats, are expected to be approved in the near future. Not all foods are suitable for this kind of treatment, however. Irradiating raw oysters, for example, damages or kills the live oysters inside the shells and actually decreases their shelf life. Irradiating raw eggs can kill any salmonella inside the shells, but it turns the egg whites milky and makes them more liquid.

Irradiated foods in the supermarket are marked by a symbol called the radura, a flower inside a broken circle. You probably will not find many of them in your local store. People have been slow to accept them, mainly because they do not know or understand what food irradiation is all about.

Irradiation helps to make foods safer, but it should not replace the usual food safety practices. First of all, the more bacteria there are in foods, the more radiation would have to be used—resulting in more changes in taste and nutritional value. Moreover, irradiation—like pasteurization—does not kill *all* the microorganisms in foods. New contamination may occur during food handling after the radiation treatment.

Dr. David A. Kessler, a former head of the FDA, says, "Some of us find the idea of irradiated food so frightening that we don't *want* to believe it's safe. But the fact is, irradiation can make our food supply safer—and that's an important goal."[3]

Government agencies will continue to monitor the food supply, helping to keep it safe. Restaurants, delis,

# Singing About Food Safety

Carl Winter grew up with a love for music. He even joined a band. After finishing college, though, Carl decided to put music behind him and concentrate on a career and family. His college degree was in toxicology, the study of poisons and their effects. After earning a Ph.D. in agricultural and environmental chemistry, he eventually became a college professor at the University of California at Davis. Research on pesticide residues and natural poisons in foods was only part of his work. He was also a talented teacher who knew how to communicate both with his students and with people in the community.

In 1996 Carl brought music back into his life. He had bought a synthesizer, which transformed him into a one-person band, and realized that music could be a powerful tool for getting his message across. Since then he has been writing funny songs about food safety, rewriting the lyrics of popular hits like the Bee Gees' "Stayin' Alive." He has produced several CDs, which have been distributed all over the world. He also goes on twenty-five to thirty tours a year, performing for audiences that include food producers, science teachers, and students from grade school to college age. His programs are a big hit and have earned him nicknames such as the Sinatra of Salmonella, the Elvis of E. coli, and the Artist Formerly Known As Prince of Pesticides.

In writing his songs, Carl draws on his scientific background and also on everyday experiences. A bad chicken dinner at a restaurant while he was touring in Georgia, for example, led to an attack of food poisoning and inspired a new song, "There'll Be a Stomachache Tonight," sung to the tune of the Eagles' hit "Heartache Tonight."[2]

Here's an excerpt from one of Carl's songs, "Stayin' Alive":

> *Well you can tell by the way I choose my food*
> *I'm a worried guy, in a cautious mood.*
> *Food safety scares, they're everywhere*
> *And they're telling me I should beware.*
> *There's pesticides, Mad Cow Disease,*
> *Sure don't put my mind at ease*
> *Biotech and MSG*
> *Messin' with my sanity.*
> *Don't want hepatitis or that gastroenteritis,*
> *I'm just stayin' alive, stayin' alive,*
> *Scrubbin' off my veggies and I'm heatin' all my*
>    *burgers*
> *Up to one-eighty-five, one-eighty-five.*
> *Ah ha ha ha, stayin' alive, stayin' alive.*

and other public eating places are also improving their safety practices. Still, you and your family, as food consumers, have an important role to play. Remember the food safety rules, and you can greatly reduce your risk of getting food poisoning.

## Questions and Answers

What is the difference between food poisoning and food-borne illness? Foodborne illness is a type of food poisoning. Many experts use *foodborne illness* to describe infections caused by microorganisms in food. Food poisoning is a more general term that also includes illness due to toxins (poisons) that may occur naturally in foods or may have been introduced from the environment. However, many people use the two terms as synonyms.

I love to eat cold pizza straight out of the refrigerator. Is it safe to eat it cold, or should I heat it up first? Yes, if it was put into the refrigerator promptly (within two hours of being cooked) and it has not been there long (less than two days). Bacteria grow quickly at room temperature. Refrigerator temperatures slow down their growth but do not stop it completely. Heating up the pizza will kill most of the bacteria in it, but it will not destroy any toxins they may have produced.

If it is okay to eat rare steak that is still pink inside, then why isn't it safe to eat a rare-cooked hamburger? A steak is a solid piece of meat. Any contamination with bacteria during handling and food preparation probably occurred only on the outside. These bacteria are killed during cooking, since even a rare steak is still heated to a high temperature on the outside. Hamburger, though, is made of small pieces of chopped meat that are all mixed together when the hamburger patties are formed. The outsides of many of these small pieces wind up inside the hamburger, and if the inside is still pink, they are not cooked well enough to kill bacteria.

If heat kills bacteria in meats, then how do I avoid eating contaminated salads? You can't heat up salad. First of all, the salad preparer should wash his or her hands. Then the vegetables should be washed thoroughly. The next important thing to remember is not to use the same cutting board or knife that was used to cut up meats, poultry, or seafood so that cross-contamination will not occur.

My favorite part of baking cookies with my mom is licking the batter afterward. Now I hear that isn't safe. Why? Cookie batter contains raw eggs, which may carry salmonella. If these bacteria get into your body, you may get food poisoning.

I want to eat a frozen pizza that's in my freezer. Parts of it have freezer burn, though. Is it safe to eat, or should I throw it out? Foods may get freezer burn if they were not wrapped tightly enough and air gets inside. The air causes chemical changes in the food, which produce leathery, dry spots in the food. Freezer burn will not make you sick, but the food may not taste as good. You can cut those parts away, and safely eat what's left.

What do I do when I go picnicking with my family and there is no place to wash my hands? You can bring along some premoistened towelettes or a hand gel sanitizer that you can buy in any supermarket. These items contain alcohol, which will kill germs on your hands.

# Food Poisoning Timeline

1600s — Wealthy Americans build icehouses to store their ice and to keep their food frozen.

1790s — Nicolas Appert, a French confectioner, develops the first canning method, by which food can be safely stored in airtight glass bottles for long periods of time.

1793 — The first reported outbreak of botulism occurs in Wildbad, Germany, after people ate contaminated blood sausages.

1806 — Nicolas Appert tests his canning method on Napoléon's army with positive results.

Early 1800s — The icebox is invented, allowing people to store food inside their homes.

1810 — Englishman Peter Durand patents the canning method based on Appert's principles, but he uses cans rather than glass bottles.

1813 — Two Englishmen, Bryan Dorkin and John Hall, set up the first commercial canning factory in England.

| 1829 | German physician Justinius Kerner publishes a report describing 230 cases of "sausage poisoning." |
|---|---|
| 1857 | French chemist Louis Pasteur demonstrates that milk turns sour because microorganisms are growing in it. |
| 1860 | Pasteur conducts experiments that use heat to kill microorganisms in beer and wine (pasteurization). |
| 1883 | Robert Koch discovers the bacterium that causes cholera. |
| 1885 | American scientist Daniel E. Salmon discovers salmonella bacteria. |
| 1895 | Belgian physician Emile van Ermengem discovers botulism bacteria. |
| Late 1800s | The first mechanical refrigerator is invented. |
| 1917 | Most major cities in the U.S. have laws requiring that milk be pasteurized. |
| 1950s | Vernon Brooks discovers that botulinum toxin type A, when injected into a muscle, blocks the release of a messenger chemical from nerves that causes muscles to contract. |

1977     Martin Skirrow isolates *Campylobacter jejuni* from patients with diarrhea.

1981     First recorded outbreak of listeriosis in the United States.

1982     First reported food poisoning outbreaks caused by *E. coli* O157:H7 in the United States.

1989     FDA approves BOTOX (*botulinum toxin* type A) for the treatment of certain eye muscle disorders.

1990     FDA approves the irradiation of poultry.

1994     First human case of infection from mad cow disease is diagnosed.

1997     FDA approves the irradiation of red meat.

2000     FDA approves the irradiation of shell eggs.

2002     First case of vCJD detected in the United States in a woman from the United Kingdom.

2003     Mad cow disease first detected in United States cattle.

2006     Outbreaks of *E. coli* O157:H7 traced to packaged spinach; new outbreaks at Taco Bell restaurants.

# For More Information

Centers for Disease Control and Prevention (CDC)
National Center for Infectious Diseases
1600 Clifton Road, NE
Atlanta, GA 30333
1-800-311-3435
http://www.cdc.gov/foodsafety

U.S. Food and Drug Administration (FDA)
Center for Food Safety and Applied Nutrition
Outreach and Information Center
5100 Paint Branch Parkway HFS-555
College Park, MD 20740-3835
1-888-SAFEFOOD (1-888-723-3366)
http://vm.cfsan.fda.gov/list.html

National Library of Medicine
MEDLINEplus
8600 Rockville Pike
Bethesda, MD 20894
1-800-338-7657
http://www.nlm.nih.gov/medlineplus

U.S. Department of Agriculture (USDA)
Food Safety and Inspection Service
Washington, D.C. 20250
http://www.fsis.usda.gov
Meat and poultry hotline:
1-888-MPHOTLINE (1-888-674-6854)

# Chapter Notes

## Chapter 1. Was It Something You Ate?

1. Conor Greene, "Food Poisoning Spread at Teacher Luncheon," *Hunterdon County Democrat* (Flemington, New Jersey) May 25, 2006, p. B-3.

2. Conor Greene, "'Thank You' Luncheon May Have Felled Staff," *Hunterdon County Democrat* (Flemington, New Jersey), May 18, 2006, pp. A-1, A-4; Conor Greene, "Food Poisoning Spread at Teacher Luncheon," May 25, 2006, p. B-3; personal interview with John Beckley, director, Meileen Acosta, epidemiologist, and Carl Rachel, public information officer of the Hunterdon County Department of Health, August 23, 2006.

3. National Institutes of Allergy and Infectious Diseases, "Foodborne Diseases," *NIAID Fact Sheet,* February 2005;<http://www.niaid.nih.gov/factsheets/foodbornedis.htm> (February 9, 2006).

## Chapter 2. Food Poisoning in History

1. Judith Walzer Leavitt, *Typhoid Mary: Captive to the Public's Health,* Boston: Beacon Press, 1996, p. 43.

2. David E. Barmes, "Health Challenges for Research in the 21st Century," *World Health Organization,* December 6, 2004, <http://www.who.int/dg/lee/speeches/2004/barmeslecture/en/> (March 6, 2006).

Chapter 3. What Is Food Poisoning?

1. Patricia Guthrie, "Aftermath of a Miracle," *The Atlanta Journal,* October 6, 1998, <http://www.aboutecoli.com/news/jack-in-the-box7.htm> (February 14, 2006).

2. Senthil Nachimuthu, et al., "Food Poisoning," updated January10,2005, <http://www.emedicine.com/med/topic807.htm> (March 13, 2006).

3. Ibid.

Chapter 4. What Causes Food Poisoning?

1. Lorraine Fraser, "Millions Watched Zoe's Final Hours," *news.telegraph,* October 29, 2000, <http://www.telegraph.co.uk/news/main.jhtml?xml=/news/2000/10/29/nbse29.xml> (March 22, 2006); Mark Kennedy, "'Why Have They Done This to Her?': Mother grieved as bright, friendly girl died the frightening, degrading death that mad-cow disease brings," June 2, 2001,<http://www.organicconsumers.org/madcow/why6201.cfm> (March 22, 2006).

2. Centers for Disease Control, "Salmonellosis, General Information," October 13, 2005, <http://www.cdc.gov/ncidod/dbmd/diseaseinfo/salmonellosis_g.htm> (March 24, 2006).

3. Ibid.

4. Centers for Disease Control and Prevention, "Campylobacter infections," October 6, 2005, <http://www.cdc.gov/ncidod/dbmd/diseaseinfo/campylobacter_t.htm> (March 27, 2006).

5. Ibid.

6. Centers for Disease Control and Prevention, "Listeriosis, General Information," October 12, 2005, <http://www.cdc.gov/ncidod/dbmd/diseaseinfo/ listeriosis_g.htm> (March 24, 2006).

7. Centers for Disease Control and Prevention, "*Escherichia coli* O157:H7," October 6, 2005, <http://www.cdc.gov/ncidod/dbmd/diseaseinfo/escheri chiacoli_g.htm> (March 24, 2006).

8. Ibid.

9. The Associated Press, "Farmers given sharp warning before outbreak," MSNBC.com, September 19, 2006, <http://www.msnbc.msn.com/id/14841731> (September 19, 2006); Julia Preston and Carolyn Marshall, "Tainted spinach sickens 100 in U.S.," *International Herald Tribune,* September 17, 2006, <http://www.iht.com/articles/2006/09/17/news/spinach. php> (September 19, 2006); Associated Press, "Wild pigs suspected as cause of E. coli outbreak,: MSNBC.com,October26,2006,<http://www.msnbc.ms n.com/id/15433871/> (December 14, 2006).

10. Centers for Disease Control and Prevention, "Shigellosis,"October13,2005,<http://www.cdc.gov/ ncidod/dbmd/diseaseinfo/shigellosis_g.htm> (March 24, 2006).

11. Centers for Disease Control and Prevention, "Botulism," October 6, 2005, <http://www.cdc.gov/ ncidod/dbmd/diseaseinfo/botulism_g.htm> (March 24, 2006).

12. Centers for Disease Control and Prevention, "Norovirus: Technical Fact Sheet," August 3, 2006, <http://www.cdc.gov/ncidod/dvrd/revb/gastro/norovir us-factsheet/htm>(September 15, 2006).

13. Centers for Disease Control and Prevention, "BSE (Bovine Spongiform Encephalopathy, or Mad CowDisease),"March15,2006,<http://www.cdc.gov/ncidod/dvrd/bse/> (March 23, 2006).

14. Centers for Disease Control and Prevention, "BSE in an Alabama cow," March 15, 2006, <http://www.cdc.gov/ncidod/dvrd/bse/news/alabama_cow_031506.htm> (March 23, 2006); Centers for Disease Control and Prevention, "Confirmed Case of Variant Creutzfeldt Jakob Disease (vCJD) in the United States in a Patient from the Middle East," November 29, 2006,<http://www.cdc.gov/ncidod/dvrd/vcjd/other/vCJD_112906.htm> (December 14, 2006).

## Chapter 5. Detection and Treatment

1. Carole Sugarman, "A Taste of Food Poisoning: She Knew All About Salmonellosis—Except What It's Really Like to Have It," *The Washington Post,* July 5, 2005, p. HE01, http://www.washingtonpost.com/wp-dyn/content/article/2005/07/04/AR2005070401225_2.html (April 11, 2006).

2. Ibid.

## Chapter 6. Food Safety

1. Patricia Talorico, "Clean It Up," *The Courier News,* January 11, 1998, pp. E-1, E-8.

2. Peter Genovese, "'Sinatra of Salmonella' sings of food safety," *The Star Ledger,* pp. 51, 56. (Words and music of many of his songs can be found on Carl's web site: http://foodsafe.ucdavis.edu/music.html)

3. Betty Holcomb, "How Safe Is Your Dinner?" *Good Housekeeping,* March 1, 2000, p. 52.

# Glossary

**antibiotics**—Medicines used to kill bacteria.

**antibodies**—Special germ-fighting chemicals produced by white blood cells.

**bacteria**—Microscopic organisms that cause harm inside the body when they multiply and produce toxins.

**botulism**—A type of foodborne illness caused by a toxin produced by the bacterium *Clostridium botulinum.* The toxin attacks the nervous system and can cause muscle weakness, paralysis, and death.

**bovine spongiform encephalopathy (BSE)**—A rare, deadly disease that affects the brain of cattle; commonly known as mad cow disease. BSE is caused by a defective protein, called a prion, transmitted through contaminated animal feed.

**campylobacteriosis**—A type of foodborne illness caused by the *Campylobacter jejuni* bacterium.

**carrier**—A person or animal that is infected with a disease but does not have any symptoms. A carrier can spread the disease-causing germ to others.

**contaminated**—Changed by contact with something bad or harmful (e.g., bacteria).

**cross-contamination**—The transfer of microorganisms from one food or person to another. Microorganisms can also be transferred to cutting boards, sponges, and countertops, and then to foods.

**dehydration**—A removal or severe loss of water. Diarrhea and vomiting can lead to dehydration of the body tissues.

**diarrhea**—Frequent soft or liquid stools (body wastes).

**digestive tract**—The tubelike passageway inside the body in which food is digested. It extends from the mouth to the anus and includes the esophagus, stomach, and intestines.

**disinfectant**—Something that kills harmful microorganisms.

**drug-resistant bacteria**—Bacteria that cannot be killed by an antibiotic.

**enzyme**—A body chemical that makes reactions go or speeds them up.

**esophagus**—The tube leading from the mouth to the stomach.

**feces**—Body wastes (undigested food matter and bacteria) formed in the large intestine.

**foodborne illness**—A sickness caused by consuming food or drink that contains certain kinds of microorganisms that live and grow inside the body; commonly called food poisoning.

**fungus** (*plural* **fungi**)—A plantlike organism that feeds on living or dead matter; includes mushrooms, molds, mildew, and yeasts.

**gene**—A chemical that carries hereditary information determining a particular trait of an organism.

**hemolytic uremic syndrome (HUS)**—A complication of *E. coli* O157:H7 infections, especially in young children. Red blood cells are destroyed, which can lead to kidney failure.

**host**—A living plant or animal that provides food and shelter for another creature.

**immune system**—The body's disease-fighting system, which includes white blood cells.

**incubation period**—The period between infection by a disease germ and the onset of symptoms.

**inflammation**—Redness, heat, and swelling that develop when tissues are damaged.

**intestines**—Coiled tubelike parts of the digestive tract, in which food is digested and food materials are absorbed.

**irradiation**—Exposing foods to radiation (high-energy, invisible waves) to kill germs.

**lactose intolerance**—A condition in which the body is unable to digest lactose, a sugar found in milk and other dairy products.

**listeriosis**—A type of foodborne illness caused by the bacterium *Listeria monocytogenes*, which can be found in vegetables, milk, cheese, meat, and seafood.

**lymph nodes**—Small masses of tissue scattered along the lymph system that contain disease-fighting cells.

**macrophages**—Disease-fighting white blood cells that can eat and digest microorganisms.

**microorganisms**—Living creatures, such as bacteria, viruses, and parasites, too small to be seen without a microscope.

**organic foods**—Crops or livestock grown without using pesticides or other chemicals.

**pasteurization**—A process in which a substance is heated to a very high temperature to kill bacteria, then quickly cooled.

**perishable**—Likely to spoil or decay.

**pesticides**—Poisonous chemicals used to get rid of insects, weeds, and other pests.

**prions**—Defective proteins known to cause neurological diseases, such as bovine spongiform encephalopathy (BSE) and Creutzfeldt-Jakob disease.

**salmonellosis**—A type of foodborne illness caused by one of the *Salmonella* bacteria.

**spore**—A resting stage of bacteria, covered with a hard, protective coat.

**stool**—Solid body wastes produced in the intestines; feces.

**toxin**—A poison.

**virus**—The smallest kind of microorganism, which cannot even be seen with an ordinary microscope.

**vomiting**—Throwing up; stomach contents are forced out through the mouth.

**white blood cells**—Jelly-like blood cells that can move through tissues and are an important part of the body's defenses.

# Further Reading

## Books

Brands, Danielle. *Salmonella.* Philadelphia: Chelsea House Publishers, 2006.

Cerexhe, Peter and John Ashton. *Risky Foods, Safer Choices.* Sydney, Australia: University of New South Wales Press Ltd, 2000.

Isle, Mick. *Everything You Need to Know About Food Poisoning.* New York: The Rosen Publishing Group, Inc., 2001.

The Learning Channel. *Spreading Menace: Salmonella Attack and the Hunger Craving.* Farmington Hills, MI: The Gale Group, Inc., 2004.

Rosaler, Maxine. *Botulism.* New York: The Rosen Publishing Group, Inc., 2004.

Rue, Nancy R. and Anna Graf Williams. *Quick Reference to Food Safety & Sanitation.* Upper Saddle River, NJ: Prentice Hall, 2003.

Scott, Elizabeth and Paul Sockett. *How to Prevent Food Poisoning.* New York: John Wiley & Sons, Inc., 1998.

## Internet Addresses

(See also **For More Information**, p. 111)

**Food Safety.gov.** *Kids, Teens, and Educators.*
<http://www.foodsafety.gov/~fsg/fsgkids.html>.

**Michigan Department of Agriculture.** *Food Safety Pages.*
<http://www.mda.state.mi.us/kids/countyfair/food/index.html>.

**U.S. Food and Drug Administration.** *Food Safety Quiz for Kids.*
<http://www.fda.gov/oc/opacom/kids/html/wash__hands.htm>.

# Index